ISAAC JEREMIAH

WELCOMES THE SABBATH

By: Lyle Thompson
Illustrations: Inbal Singer

Library of Congress Cataloging ISBN: 978-1434812681

This book is dedicated to yitzchak yirmiyahu... a wonderful little boy who will certainly inspire many people in his lifetime...

– Zaida Lyle

For A.J., for believing in me.

– I.S.

It was late Friday afternoon.

The house had been cleaned, the meals had been prepared and the table had been set with a white tablecloth and special dishes. Everyone was getting ready to welcome the Sabbath.

Suddenly the silence was broken with the cries of two year old Isaac Jeremiah.

"Eema! Eema! Story! Story! Israel! Israel!"

"Ok, but it will have to be a quick story Isaac Jeremiah, because it is almost time to welcome the Sabbath," said Eema.
He climbed up on to Eema's lap.

"Once upon a time, when Isaac Jeremiah was just a baby, we all lived in an apartment in a beautiful little hillside city in Israel called Ramat Beit Shemesh.

Isaac Jeremiah had just learned to stand and he loved to blow kisses and give "high fives". His hair was getting long as it had never been cut and he was just starting to wear a kippa.

Every day after morning prayers, Abba would go to yeshiva to study. Isaac Jeremiah would stay at home with Eema.

In the morning, he played with his toys and helped Eema clean up the apartment. Then they listened to music and played musical instruments.

After lunch, Isaac Jeremiah and Eema would go to the park and play on the toys with other little boys and girls. He especially liked to play in the sand, go on the slide and ride on the merry-go-round.

When Abba came home from yeshiva it was time for supper. Isaac Jeremiah really liked to eat fresh fruit. He squished the food in his hand and would even throw some of it on the floor to see if it would stick.

Every night, before bed, Isaac Jeremiah would get a bath. It was a very fun time for him as he splashed and played with his toys in the bathtub.

His favorite toy was a yellow rubber ducky. Abba usually dried him off with a big towel and then put him to bed and read him a story. Afterwards, Abba had to clean up the mess in the bathroom.

On Thursday night after dinner and evening prayers, Abba and Eema and Isaac Jeremiah would clean up the apartment in preparation of the Sabbath.

They had to put away all the toys, vacuum, wash the floor, dust and make everything very clean. After Isaac Jeremiah went to sleep, Abba and Eema would do all the cooking for the Sabbath.

Early on Friday morning, Abba would load everyone in to the car and drive to Jerusalem. The first stop was always the Old City, where Abba, Eema and Isaac Jeremiah would go and pray at the Western Wall. There were always a lot of people there from all over the world and Issac Jeremiah was always a big hit. Abba and Issac Jeremiah went to pray on the left side and Eema went to pray on the right side.

After praying at the Western Wall, the family went to the Shuk in Jerusalem to buy challah, fresh fruit and vegetables and Abba's favorite dessert for the Sabbath. Abba really liked those "rugalach," didn't he?

rugalach

The Shuk was always very crowded and there were many vendors yelling out about their special deals:

"Get your apples here!
Get your oranges here!
Get your pears here!"

Eema always looked for a needy person asking for money so she can donate 'tsadaka'. Usually there was a woman with her young children sitting on the sidewalk and Eema liked to donate to her.

The family then jumped back in the car and Abba quickly drove back to Ramat Beit Shemesh as the sun was now low in the sky.

When they arrived back in the apartment, everyone helped set up the Sabbath table. Usually, several boys from the yeshiva came to stay with the family for the weekend and to celebrate the Sabbath.

Isaac Jeremiah liked having visitors since he got lots of attention, got to show them his "high fives" and sing and dance.

Everyone would get all dressed up and at sundown, after Abba had gone to the synagogue, Eema and Isaac Jeremiah would light two Sabbath candles: one to "remember" the Sabbath and one to "observe" it. Eema would then cover her eyes with her hands and say a special blessing.

When Abba came back from the synagogue, everyone would gather around the table and sing "Shalom Aleichem". You loved singing.

Abba would then say the "Kiddush" using grape juice in a special cup and then Abba and Eema would say a special prayer just for you.

We would then all go into the kitchen to wash our hands in a special way, saying a special prayer. We had to remember not to say anything until after we ate the challah, and this wasn't very easy was it?

We always had two challah loaves covered on the Sabbath table. These represented the double portion that the children of Israel gathered on Fridays when they were in the dessert. Abba would then remove the cover and say the "Motzi" blessing over the bread.

During the meal, Abba would often discuss the Torah or lessons he had learned that week and we would sing songs.

After the meal we would "bentch", saying the Birkat Hamazon. We would then sing and read some of your books before it was time for your bed.

On Saturday mornings, the family would go to the synagogue. After morning prayers at the synagogue everyone returned to the apartment for the noon meal. After the meal, the family played some games and went for a walk to the park.

At sundown, on Saturday, Abba would lead us in a "Havdalah" ceremony to end the Sabbath. You always liked watching Abba douse the candle in the wine.

After Havdalah, the Sabbath was over for another week. The boys went back to the yeshiva and Isaac Jeremiah got to play in the bath and head to bed after a nice story from Abba.

And that was how we celebrated the Sabbath in Israel."

Suddenly, Eema realized the sun was setting and it was time to light the candles, say the prayers and welcome the Sabbath....

THE END

482405